TO THE BENDING SKY

TO THE BENDING SKY

*Poems of
Julia Dorr*

Burlington, Vermont

Introduction and design © Rutland Free Library, 2022
Illustrations © Bianca Amira Zanella, 2022
Cover design by Chris Booth, Vibe Portrait Art

Onion River Press
191 Bank Street
Burlington, VT 05401

ISBN: 978-1-949066-95-1 paperback

Contents

Introduction	1

SUMMER JOY

Over the Wall	7
Three Songs	10
The Mountain Road	11
Jacques and Suzette	14
A Summer Song	17
A Class Poem	19
Moon Pictures	22
The Joy	24
Afternoon	26
To A Dandelion	29
Without and Within	31
The Comrades: The Soul to the Body	34

WINTER RESILIENCE

An Afterthought: The Body to the Soul	39
What My Friend Said To Me	42
Two Paths	43
Come What May	44
The Choice	46
Spirit To Spirit	48
Remembrance	50
The Countersign	51
Outgrown	52
When Dreams Depart	55
"Only"	56
When Lesser Loves	57
A Night Reverie	58

Introduction

Julia C.R. Dorr (1825-1913) has a lasting legacy not only in the community of Rutland, Vermont, but in the larger literary world of New England poets. Her friendships and literary peers included well-recognized names such as Henry Wadsworth Longfellow, Oliver Wendell Holmes, Ralph Waldo Emerson, and others. She frequently hosted poets at her Rutland home "The Maples," and many considered her a cherished friend as well as a woman author of rare power.

While individuals remembered in history are typically distinguished by either word or deed, Julia's legacy has the rare distinction of spanning both. She brought the same soft humility of spirit, gratitude, and deep wonder to her philanthropic efforts as she did to her prolific written work. As a writer, she penned novels, travel memoirs, and a book of guidance for newlyweds; however, it is her poetry for which she is best known.

Lyrical, playful, and keenly insightful, her poems draw heavily from her sense of spiritual place to reflect to readers a world full of meaning, beauty, and wonder. Although she frequently uses religious imagery to express her ideas, her faith was larger than any specific sect. She references deities and mythical figures across cultures with the same reverence and awe. In truth, Nature for her was deified. Her God was any god, any tree, any root. Late into her life, she maintained a habit of wearing a rose from her garden as a physical reminder of her sense of divine connection, a "garden" both internal and external. She found deep solace in the larger cycles of the seasons, often completing the cycle of growth and decline within a single poem. Even in her more darkly reflective poems, she often circled back to the idea of being only a small part of a vast and loving cosmos. Her spirit itself was vast. Her work, like herself, resilient.

The strong, inner flame evident in her poetry led her to found Rutland Free Library in 1886. 136 years later, the Rutland Free Library is proud to continue Julia's legacy of community building and service. With this volume, we are honored to give Julia's words back to the community she loved so deeply, and to celebrate her work and spirit.

—Amy Williams, Assistant Director of
The Rutland Free Library, August 2021

This volume of selected poetry coincides with the ninth sculpture installation of the Rutland Sculpture Trail Series, honoring Julia Dorr, and incorporates 14 motifs from her poem "Over the Wall." This widespread, heartfelt effort has been made possible through the gifts of many community members, including: The Carving Studio & Sculpture Center, Green Mountain Power, MKF Properties, and Vermont Quarries for collaboratively creating the Rutland Sculpture Trail initiative. Leaders of the Dorr sculpture include Steve Costello; donors Mary Moran, Mary Powell, and Joan Gamble; Amanda Sisk, sculpture designer, and Evan Morse and Taylor Apostol, sculptors.

Gratitude to those who worked to bring this volume to manifestation:

Amanda Sisk, who provided great insight into Julia Dorr's relationship to her world;

Bianca Amira Zanella, passionate Rutland poet whose eye, ear, technical knowledge, and insight have been vital to creating this collection. Her roses illustrate each section of this volume;

Will Notte, State Representative, RFL Board member, and manager of Phoenix Books, Rutland, who had the idea to publish this volume and helped get it to press;

Chris Booth, photographer and artist, for his creative input and cover design;

Barry Cohen, RFL Board Treasurer and community activist who propelled this wonderful idea forward into physical reality.

Summer Joy

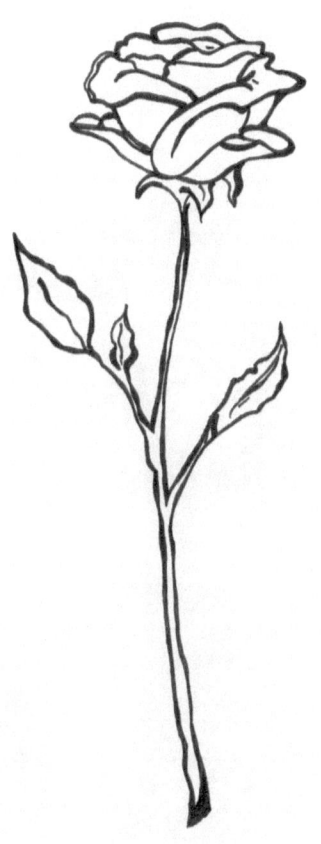

Over the Wall

I know a spot where the wild vines creep,
    And the coral moss-cups grow,
And where, at the foot of the rocky steep,
    The sweet blue violets blow.
There all day long, in the summer-time,
You may hear the river's dreamy rhyme;
There all day long does the honey-bee
Murmur and hum in the hollow tree.

And there the feathery hemlock makes
    A shadow cool and sweet,
While from its emerald wing it shakes
    Rare incense at your feet.
There do the silvery lichens cling,
There does the tremulous harebell swing;
And many a scarlet berry shines
Deep in the green of the tangled vines.

Over the wall at dawn of day,
    Over the wall at noon,
Over the wall when the shadows say
    That night is coming soon,
A little maiden with laughing eyes
Climbs in her eager haste, and hies
Down to the spot where the wild vines creep,
And violets bloom by the rocky steep.

All wild things love her. The murmuring bee
    Scarce stirs when she draws near,
And sings the bird in the hemlock-tree
    Its sweetest for her ear.
The harebells nod as she passes by,
The violet lifts its tender eye,
The low ferns bend her steps to greet,
And the mosses creep to her dancing feet.

Up in her pathway seems to spring
    All that is sweet or rare,—
Chrysalis quaint, or the moth's bright wing,
    Or flower-buds strangely fair.
She watches the tiniest bird's-nest hid
The thickly clustering leaves amid;
And the small brown tree-toad on her arm
Quietly hops, and fears no harm.

Ah, child of the laughing eyes, and heart
    Attuned to Nature's voice!
Thou hast found a bliss that will ne'er depart
    While earth can say, "Rejoice!"
The years must come, and the years must go;
But the flowers will bloom, and the breezes blow,
And bird and butterfly, moth and bee,
Bring on their swift wings joy to thee!

Three Songs

Sing me a song of Living,
    Exultant, strong and clear;
A song of the joy of Being,
    Rolling from sphere to sphere;
A song that the choiring angels
    Might lean from heaven to hear!

Sing me a song of Loving,
    Tenderly, sweet and low;
Sing of its rose-flushed dawning
    And its lingering sunset glow
Of its heart like a ruby flaming
    In the depths of the Alpine snow!

Sing me a song of Triumph
    Over the mists of death;
Over the deepening shadows;
    Over the failing breath;
Over the lonely valley
    Where no voice answereth!

The Mountain Road

Only a glimpse of mountain road
That followed where a river flowed;
Only a glimpse—then on we passed
Skirting the forest dim and vast.

I closed my eyes. On rushed the train
Into the dark, then out again,
Startling the song-birds as it flew
The wild ravines and gorges through.

But, heeding not the dangerous way
O'erhung by sheer cliffs, rough and gray,
I only saw, as in a dream,
The road beside the mountain stream.

No smoke curled upward in the air,
No meadow-lands stretched broad and fair;
But towering peaks rose far and high,
Piercing the clear, untroubled sky.

Yet down the yellow, winding road
That followed where the river flowed,
I saw a long procession pass
As shadows over bending grass.

The young, the old, the sad, the gay,
Whose feet had worn that narrow way,
Since first within the dusky glade
Some Indian lover wooed his maid;

Or silent crept from tree to tree—
Spirit of stealthy vengeance, he!
Or breathless crouched while through the brake
The wild deer stole his thirst to slake.

The barefoot school-boys rushing out,
An eager, crowding, roisterous rout;
The sturdy lads; the lassies gay
As bobolinks in merry May;

The farmer whistling to his team
When first the dawn begins to gleam;
The loaded wains that one by one
Drag slowly home at set of sun;

Young lovers straying hand in hand
Within a fair, enchanted land;
And many a bride with lingering feet;
And many a matron calm and sweet;

And many an old man bent with pain;
And many a solemn funeral train;
And sometimes, red against the sky,
An army's banners waving high!

All mysteries of life and death
To which the spirit answereth,
Are thine, O lonely mountain road,
That followed where the river flowed!

Jacques and Suzette

There you sit in a niche together,
Out of the reach of wind and weather,
Looking down on a fierce bronze dragon,
A cloisonné vase, and a gilded flagon,
The opal gleam of a Venice glass,
A chamois climbing an Alpine pass,
An ivory boat from far Japan,
An odorous flask from Ispahan,
      And a host of things–
Trifles that last while Life takes wings!

O chère Suzette, what years have flown
Since you and Jacques were together thrown,
And loved and quarreled, and loved again–
The old, old fate of dames and men!
But there you sit in your carven shrine,
With never a thought of me or mine,
      Even though beset
By your great-great-grandchildren, belle Suzette!

Puffed and powdered your golden hair
Gleaming under the rose you wear,
One long, loose curl dropping low
Over your bosom's tender snow;
Arching eyebrows, and smiling lips
Red as the rose the wild bee sips–
    Thus, even yet,
I see and I know you, chère Suzette!

White puffed sleeves and a fall of lace,
Lending your figure girlish grace;
Purple bodice the gems bedeck;
A string of amethysts round your neck;
Plenty of furbelows to show
How you plumed your gay wings long ago,
    Lady Suzette,
In the days when youth and pleasure met.

But, Grand-père Jacques with your curled brown
    Wig,
And your broad white kerchief, trim, and trig,
Out of which rises your shaven chin,
With your delicate lips and your nostrils thin,
And a certain self-confident, high-bred air,
Smiling and gallant and debonair–
    I wonder yet
If she made your heart ache, this Suzette?

Or perhaps, monsieur, 'twas the other way;
For she was jealous and you were gay,
And under that frill of falling snow
A passionate heart beat warm, I know
Dear Grand-père Jacques, I doubt if you
Were undeniably good and true;
  Did you make her fret,
Though you called her gently, "Ma chère
  Suzette"?

Ye do not answer, O smiling lips!
From the silent past no answer slips.
Quaint letter more than a century old
Hint at romances that might be told;
But dust and ashes are all who knew
How life fared on between you two,
  Jacques and Suzette,
Or how its warp and its woof were set.

Nay, nay, dear hearts, I will vex you not;
Be your loves, or glad or sad, forgot!
Keep ye your secrets an you will,
Sitting up yonder calm and still,
Side by side in a niche together,
Out of the reach of stormy weather,
  And whispering yet,
"Mon ami Jacques!" "Ma chère Suzette!"

A Summer Song

Roly-poly honey-bee,
    Humming in the clover,
Under you the tossing leaves,
    And the blue sky over,
Why are you so busy, pray?
    Never still a minute,
Hovering now above a flower,
    Now half-buried in it!

Jaunty robin-redbreast,
    Singing loud and cheerly,
From the pink-white apple tree
    In the morning early,
Tell me, is your merry song
    Just for your own pleasure,
Poured from such a tiny throat,
    Without stint or measure?

Little yellow buttercup,
    By the way-side smiling,
Lifting up your happy face,
    With such sweet beguiling,
Why are you so gayly clad—
    Cloth of gold your raiment?
Do the sunshine and the dew
    Look to you for payment?

Roses in the garden beds,
    Lilies, cool and saintly,
Darling blue-eyed violets,
    Pansies, hooded quaintly,
Sweet-peas that, like butterflies,
    Dance the bright skies under,
Bloom ye for your own delight,
    Or for ours, I wonder!

A Class Poem

Fair girls, with your sunlit faces
    Turned to the morning skies,
With your lips attuned to laughter,
    And the young light in your eyes,
What message shall I bring you
    From the far Mount of Years?
Shall it be song or sermon?
    A thing of smiles or tears?

You know not yet what life is;
    Its heart's-ease and its rue,
Its bitter-sweet and golden-rod
    Have blossomed not for you.
You have but plucked the wild rose
    Blooming beside the way,
And heard the thrushes' love song
    Borne on the winds of May.

Ah, well I know the wonder
    And the glory of it all,
And how your hearts are bounding
    As at the trumpet's call!
I know your dreams and visions
    Of the life that is to be—
The glamour of moon and starlight,
    The magic of cloud and sea!

To dream is sweet. But sweeter,
    Dear hearts, the awakening is;
I, who have dreamed and wakened,
    I joy to tell you this.
Illusion's frail white blossom
    May fade as climbs the sun,
But the same sun ripens fruitage
    Fairer to look upon.

For— Doing is better than Dreaming;
    August is richer than June;
And the harvester's chant of labor
    Is set to a nobler tune.
Yet— Being is better than Doing!
    Hark! How the music swells
As the pageant of life sweeps onward
    To the pealing of mighty bells!

And when Endeavor is over,
    As it must be, soon or late,
It is good to sit in the twilight
    With folded hands and wait.
It is good to know that the sowing
    And the reaping all are done,
And to learn that the star of evening
    Shines clear as the rising sun!

Moon Pictures

A slender crescent in the opal west,
Low-hung above a mountain's darkening crest–
A silent dream above a world at rest.

....

The bending curve of the horizon bar–
A silver boat moored high in depths afar,
Cradling in tender arms one lone bright star!

....

An orchard close where wandering moonbeams strayed,
Weaving weird tapestries of light and shade,
And fairy paths for fairy footsteps made.

....

A great white harvest moon, divinely fair,
Slow sailing through resplendent seas of air,
Over dark pine-trees, and a garden rare.

....

A broad street flooded with the silver flow
Of the white moonbeams on new-fallen snow,
While, overhead, cloud shapes swept to and fro;

....

A curtained window and a casement low,
And a fair woman in the radiant glow
On whom the king smiled, passing, long ago!

....

The Joy

The joy is in the doing,
    Not the deed that's done;
The swift and glad pursuing,
    Not the goal that's won.

The joy is in the seeing,
    Not in what we see;
The ecstasy of vision,
    Far and clear and free!

The joy is in the singing,
    Whether heard or no;
The poet's wild, sweet rapture,
    And song's divinest flow!

The joy is in the being-
    Joy of life and breath;
Joy of a soul triumphant,
    Conqueror of death!

Is there a flaw in the marble?
    Sculptor, do your best;
The joy is in the endeavor.
    Leave to God the rest!

Afternoon

O perfect day,
I bid thee stay!
Too fast thy glad hours slip away;
The morn, the noon,
Have fled too soon—
Delay, O golden afternoon!

O peerless Sun,
Thou radiant one
Whose dazzling course is half-way run,
Stay, stay thy flight
Down yon blue height,
Nor haste thee to the arms of night!

The west wind blows
O'er beds of rose,
But does not stir my deep repose.
In dreamful guise
I close mine eyes,
Borne on its wings to Paradise.

Beneath this tree
Half consciously
I share the life of all things free,
Hearing the beat
Of rhythmic feet,
As the grasses run my hand to meet.

The wild bee's hum,
The lone bird's drum,
O'er the wide pastures faintly come;
And soft and clear
Falls on my ear
The cow-bell's tinkle, far and near!

Before my eyes
Three blue peaks rise,
Piercing the bright autumnal skies;
Silent and grand,
On either hand,
Far mountain heights majestic stand.

By wreaths of mist
The vales are kissed—
Fair, floating clouds of amethyst,
That follow on,
Through shade and sun,
Where'er the river's course may run.

Here, looking down
On roof-trees brown,
I catch fair glimpses of the town.
There, far away,
The shadows play
On crags and bowlders, huge and gray.

All whispering low,
The breezes go—
The wandering birds flit to and fro;
Winged motes float by
Me as I lie,
And yellow leaves drop silently.

The morn, the noon,
Have fled too soon—
Delay, O golden afternoon,
While with rapt eyes
My spirit flies
From yon blue peaks to Paradise!

To A Dandelion

Little golden Dandelion,
　　Shining in the sun,
All the birds are singing now,
　　Day is just begun.
Grasses spring to greet thee;
　　Joy is everywhere,
Light and song and fragrance
　　Filling all the air!

Pallid, white-haired Dandelion,
　　Swaying in the sun,
Tall and slender, silver-crowned,
　　Day is well-nigh done!
Fair and frail, O phantom,
　　Thou art but a theme
For a minstrel's singing
　　Or a poet's dream!

Lo! A breeze sweeps by thee!
    Wither art thou flown?
All thy silver tresses
    To the winds are blown!
Whither now hath vanished
    All thy slender grace,
All the starlike beauty
    Of thy perfect face?

Gone, all gone forever!
    Nay— another spring
Glad earth shall be gay again
    With thy blossoming.
Death is life, —and life is joy!
    Sleep in peace awhile,
Till thou wakest, young and fair,
    In the Day-God's smile!

Without and Within

Softly the gold has faded from the sky,
    Slowly the stars have gathered one by one,
Calmly the crescent moon mounts up on high,
    And the long day is done.

With quiet heart my garden-walks I tread,
    Feeling the beauty that I cannot see;
Beauty and fragrance all around me shed
    By flower, and shrub, and tree.

Often I linger where the roses pour
    Exquisite odors from each glowing cup;
Or where the violet, brimmed with sweetness o'er,
    Lifts its small chalice up.

With fragrant breath the lilies woo me now,
    And softly speaks the sweet-voiced mignonette,
While heliotropes, with meekly lifted brow,
    Say to me, "Go not yet."

So for awhile I linger, but not long.
    High in the heavens rideth fiery Mars,
Careering proudly 'mid the glorious throng,
    Brightest of all the stars.

But softly gleaming through the curtain's fold,
    The home-star beams with more alluring ray,
And, as a star led sage and seer of old,
    So it directs my way;

And leads me in where my young children lie,
    Rosy and beautiful in tranquil rest;
The seal of sleep is on each fast-shut eye,
    Heaven's peace within each breast.

I bring them gifts. Not frankincense nor myrrh—
    Gifts the adoring Magi humbly brought
The young child, cradled in the arms of her
    Blest beyond mortal thought;

But love—the love that fills my mother-heart
    With a sweet rapture oft akin to pain;
Such yearning love as bids the tear-drops start
    And fall like summer rain.

And faith—that dares, for their dear sakes, to climb
    Boldly, where once it would have feared to go,
And calmly standing upon heights sublime,
    Fears not the storm below.

And prayer! O God! unto thy throne I come,
    Bringing my darlings—but I cannot speak.
With love and awe oppressed, my lips are dumb:
    Grant what my heart would seek!

The Comrades: The Soul to the Body

Comrade, art thou weary?
    Hath the way been long?
Dost thou faint and falter—
    Thou, who wert so strong?

Ah, I well remember
    How, when life was young,
Forth we fared together,
Glad of heart and tongue.

Then no height appalled thee;
    Thou didst mount and sing
With the joyous ardor
    Of a bird on wing!

Once thou wert the stronger—
    Led me by thy will;
I obeyed thy mandates,
    Gloried in thy skill;

Owed thee much, and loved thee,
>   Half the joy of living
> (Comrade, dost thou hear me?)
> Hath been of thy giving.

Think what thou has brought me!
>   All that eye hath seen—
> Glow of dawn and sunset;
>   Starlight's silver sheen;

All the pomp and splendor
>   Of the summer day;
> Gleam of sparkling waters
>   Leaping in their play;

Night and storm and darkness;
>   Mountains high and hoar
> Ocean billows sweeping
>   On from shore to shore!

Think of what I owe thee!
>   Fragrance of the rose,
> Breath of odorous lily
>   And each flower that blows;

Song of thrush and veery
>   Deep in woodland bowers;
> Chime of sweet bells pealing
>   From cathedral towers;

Love's most dear caresses,
  Touch of lip and cheek,
Throb of heart revealing
  What no tongue can speak!

Lifelong friend and comrade,
  Twin-born brother, thou,
Think how thou hast served me—
  Let me serve thee now!

Let my strength uphold thee
  As thine own strength fails,
As the way grows steeper
  And the night prevails.

Cheer thee, cheer thee, comrade!
  Drink thou of my wine;
Lo! The cup I bring thee
  Holds a draught divine!

Winter Resilience

An Afterthought: The Body to the Soul

Together still, old comrade—thou and I!
    From out the dark, drear places,
    The awful, rayless spaces,
Where only storms and dreadful shapes swept by,
    We have come forth again
    Into the world of men,
Have seen the darkness vanish, and the day
    Drive night away?

Art thou not glad? Is it not good to be
    Alive on this green earth,
    This realm of home and hearth?
Is it not good for thee as well as me?
    Oh, earth is warm and dear;
    Its touch is close and near;
And the unknown is cold and dim, and far
    As any star!

Speak thou, O soul! Art thou not glad to-day
    That we are still together
    In the clear summer weather?
Can we see the shadows on the mountains play,
    The glory of the trees
    The splendor of the seas,
The pomp of dawn and sunset, and the fair
    Blue fields of air?

Hark, how the birds are singing! And I hear
    From shrub and flower and tree
    The humming of the bee,
Nature's melodious chanting soft and clear,
    The breath of winds that pass
    Over the bending grass,
Childhood's blithe laughter, and the sweet
    Fall of its feet!

Thank God! Thank God! Comrade, rejoice with me
    In that I am still here
    Where life and love are dear,
And as of old clasp loyal hands with thee!
    And yet— and yet—
    I cannot quite forget
That thou didst fail me in mine hour of need,
    Nor gave me heed!

Ah, wither didst thou flee what time I lay
        In the unfathomed dark?
        Soul didst thou find an ark
Secure and safe until the dawn of day,
        Forgetting thou hadst sworn
        An oath not yet outworn,
To stay me with thy strength, to bring me wine
        From hills divine?

But – I forgive thee! It may be that thou,
        Even as I, wert bound
        Beyond all ken, or sound,
Or faintest memory of earthly vow.
        So, hand in hand, old friend,
        Until the path shall end,
We will fare on together, thou and I,
        Counting the stars on high!

What My Friend Said To Me

Trouble? dear friend, I know her not. God sent
    His angel Sorrow on my heart to lay
    Her hand in benediction, and to say,
"Restore, O child, that which thy Father lent,
For He doth now recall it," long ago.
    His blessed angel Sorrow! She has walked
    For years beside me, and we two have talked
As chosen friends together. Thus I know
Trouble and Sorrow are not near of kin.
    Trouble distrusteth God, and ever wears
    Upon her brow the seal of many cares;
But Sorrow oft hast deepest peace within.
    She sits with Patience in perpetual calm,
    Waiting till Heaven shall send the healing balm.

Two Paths

A Path across a meadow fair and sweet,
Where clover-blooms the lithesome grasses greet,
A path worn smooth by his impetuous feet.

A straight, swift path—and at its end, a star
Gleaming behind the lilac's fragrant bar,
And her soft eyes, more luminous by far !
....
A path across the meadow fair and sweet,
Still sweet and fair where blooms and grasses meet—
A path worn smooth by his reluctant feet.

A long, straight path—and, at its end, a gate
Behind whose bars she doth in silence wait
To keep the tryst, if he comes soon or late !

Come What May

   Come what may—
Though what remaineth I may not know,
Nor how many times the rose may blow
For my delight, or whether the years
Shall be set to the chime of falling tears,
   Or go on their way rejoicing—
  Yet, come what may,
  I have had my day!

   Come what may—
The lurid storm or the sunset peace,
The lingering pain or the swift release,
Lonely vigils and watchings long,
Passionate prayer or soaring song,
   Or silence deep and golden—
  Still, come what may,
  I have had my day!

Come what may,
I have known the fiery heart of youth,
Its rapturous joy, its bitter ruth;
I have felt the thrill of the eager doer,
The quick heart-throb of the swift pursuer,
　　The flush of glad possession—
　And, come what may,
　I have had my day!

　　Come what may,
I have learned that out of the night is born
The mystic flower of the early morn;
I have learned that after the frost of pain
The lily of peace will bloom again,
　　And the rose of consolation.
　Then, come what may,
　I have had my day!

The Choice

A voice came down from regions far away,
    Solemn and stern, yet most divinely sweet,
    "Choose thou, O Soul, the pathway for thy feet
When thou art done with Earth's bewildering day!
The high gods speak through me. They bid me say
    When thou no more shalt hear life's surges beat
    Upon the shores of time, nor wake to greet
The glorious morn, high noon, nor twilight gray.

    "They give thee leave to choose thy destiny.
    Wilt live again in some new sphere, or go
    Through the strange paths the living may not know
To utter nothingness?—Yet hear thou me
Ere thou decides, for the gods decree
    Who lives immortally shall never sow
    In the new soil the seeds of earthly woe,
Of earthly love, or earthly memory."

And thus I answered: "Give me leave to die
    Once and forever, ye who ne'er have known
    The might of human love, nor shared its throne,
Tasted its bread and wine, nor lifted high
Its royal banners to the bending sky.
    Too sweet, too strong Earth's tender loves have
        Grown!
    Rather than life whence their dear ghosts have
flown,
    O ye who are immortal, let me die!

Spirit To Spirit

Eons, or centuries, or years ago—
    We two were man and woman, thou and I,
On yon dear earth now swinging far below
    That star-mists floating by.

But now we are two spirits, in the wide
    Mysterious realm whereof all mortals dream;
The unknown country where the dead abide
    Beyond the sunset gleam.

And I—I cannot find thee anywhere!
    I roam from star to star in search of thee;
I wander through the boundless fields of air,
    And by the crystal sea.

I scan all faces and I question all;
    I breathe thy name to every wind that blows;
Through the wide silences I call and call—
    But still the silence grows.

Dost thou remember how, one midnight drear,
  We sat before a fading fire alone,
Dreaming young dreams the while the wan old year
  Reeled from his trembling throne?

And thou didst whisper, "Dear, from farthest skies,
  From utmost space, my love shall summon thee,
Though the grave-mould lie darkly on thine eyes,
  To keep this tryst with me!"

Was it last year?   O Love, I do not know!
  The high gods count not time.   We are as they.
All silently the tides of being flow;
  A year is as a day!

I only know I cannot find thee, dear!
  This might universe is all too wide;
Where art thou? In what far-removed sphere
  Is thought of me denied?

New lives, new loves, new knowledge, and new laws!
  I still remember. Does thy soul forget?
Heart unto heart if love no longer draws,
  Then the last seal is set!

Remembrance

I do remind me how, when, by a bier,
    I looked my last on an unanswering face
    Serenely waiting for the grave's embrace,
One who would fain have comforted said: "Dear,
This is the worst. Life's bitterest drop is here.
    Impartial fate has done you this one grace,
    That till you go to your appointed place,
Or soon or late, there is no more to fear."
It was not true, my soul! it was not true!
    "Thou art not lost while I remember thee,
    Lover and friend!" I cry, with bated breath.
What if the years, slow-creeping like the blue,
Resistless tide, should blot that face from me?
    Not to remember would be worse than death!

The Countersign

How shall I know thee when we two shall meet
    In the vast spaces where the dead abide?
    Never on earth shall we stand side by side.
I have not heard thy voice, nor the quick beat
Of thy glad footsteps in the hurrying street;
    Nor have I seen thy face; nor, in the wide,
    Deep silences where prayer is justified,
Have we two knelt God's dear love to entreat.
Then by what strange, mysterious countersign,
    What mystic shibboleth, will thy strong soul
        Recognize mine in that transcendent hour
When, face to face on some fair mount divine,
    We see far off the might planets roll,
        Love and immortal life our deathless dower?

Outgrown

Nay, you wrong her, my friend, she's not fickle; her love
    she has simply outgrown;
One can read the whole matter, translating her heart by
    the light of one's own.

Can you bear me to talk with you frankly? There is much
    that my heart would say,
And you know we were children together, have quarreled
    and "made up" in play.

And so, for the sake of old friendship, I venture to tell you
    the truth,
As plainly, perhaps, and as bluntly, as I might in our
    earlier youth.

Five summers ago, when you wooed her, you stood on the
    self-same plane,
Face to face, heart to heart, never dreaming your souls
    could be parted again.

She loved you at that time entirely, in the bloom of her
    life's early May,
And it is not her fault, I repeat it, that she does not love
    you to-day.

Nature never stands still, nor souls either. They ever go up
    or go down;
And hers has been steadily soaring,—but how has it been
    with your own?

She has struggled, and yearned, and aspired,—grown
    stronger and wiser each year;
The stars are not farther above you, in yon luminous
    atmosphere!

For she whom you crowned with fresh roses, down yonder,
    five summers ago,
Has learned that the first of our duties to God and
    ourselves is to grow.

Her eyes they are sweeter and calmer, but their vision is
    clearer as well;
Her voice has a tenderer cadence, but it rings like a silver
    bell.

Her face has the look worn by those who with God and his
    angels have talked;
The white robes she wears are less white than the spirits
    with whom she has walked.

And you? Have you aimed at the highest? Have you,
>   too, aspired and prayed?
Have you looked upon evil unsullied? have you conquered
>   it undismayed?

Have you, too, grown stronger and wiser, as the months
>   and the years have rolled on?
Did you meet her this morning rejoicing in the triumph of
>   victory won?

Nay, hear me! The truth cannot harm you. When to-day
>   in her presence you stood,
Was the hand that you gave her as white and clean as that
>   of her womanhood?

Go measure yourself by her standard. Look back on the
>   years that have fled;
Then ask, if you need, why she tells you that the love of her
>   girlhood is dead!

She cannot look down to her lover; her love, like her soul,
>   aspires;
He must stand by her side, or above her, who would kindle
>   its holy fires.

Now, farewell! For the sake of old friendship I have
>   ventured to tell you the truth,
As plainly, perhaps, and as bluntly, as I might in our
>   earlier youth.

When Dreams Depart

When dreams depart, then it is time to die.
    Nay, thou art dead when thy dear dreams depart,
    Even though thy ghost still haunts the crowded mart,
Still with proud grace salutes the passer-by,
Reaps golden grain when the hot sun rides high,
    Sails the far seas with compass and chart,
    Of the world's burdens bears its wonted part,
Or faces doom with calm, undaunted eye.
For dreams—they are the very breath of life;
    The "little leaven" that informs the whole;
        Wine of the gods, poured from the upper skies;
Manna from heaven, to nerve thee for the strife.
    Fetter thy dreams and hold them fast, O soul!
        When they depart, it is thyself that dies.

"Only"

Only a footstep at the door;
    A shadow on the wall;
Fine courtesies; some tender words—
    And that was all!

Only a dream that ne'er came true;
    Yet held the heart in thrall;
A memory that would not die—
    And that was all!

Only a wistful face whereon
    Time's deepening shadows fall;
A heart-cry for what never was—
    And that is all!

When Lesser Loves

When lesser loves by the relentless flow
    Of mighty currents from my arms were torn
    And swept, unheeding, to that silent bourn
Whose mystic shades no living man may know,
By night, by day, I sang my songs; and so,
    Out of the sackcloth that my soul had worn,
    Weaving my purple, I forgot to mourn,
Pouring my grief out in melodious woe!
Now am I dumb, dear heart. My lips are mute.
    Yet if from yonder blue height thou dost lean
    Earthward, remembering love's last wordless kiss,
Know thou no trembling thrills of harp or lute,
    Dying soft wails and tender songs between,
    Were half so voiceful as this silence is!

A Night Reverie

Now day is done, and heart and hand may rest!
The calm of night is on the dreaming earth;
The soft winds sleep, and faintly from afar
The night-bird's lone and melancholy cry
Makes the wide silence deeper.   Stealthily
The noiseless shadows creep from tree to tree;
All silently the darkling river flows;
All quietly the watching stars look down
On hills and valleys wrapped in deep repose.

   O hush, hush, hush!   It is the time of prayer—
The time for visions—and the hour for dreams!
Breathe thou no whisper.   Let no voice profane
The holy silences of earth and heaven.

   Darker and darker still!   The mighty dome
Of yon great maple lifts itself on high
In worship of the Infinite.   Then a glow
Fainter than that of dawning steals athwart
The lower heavens, and earth, breathless, waits
Moment by moment, till the mountain peaks
Startled from slumber put their glory on-
And lo!   The harvest moon!

                            Thou glorious one!

Shall frail man call thee *dead*, thou who hast seen
Eons and cycles pass, and centuries
Seek one by one the bourn whence none returns,
And generation after generation fall
As falls the grass before the mower's scythe,
To die and be forgotten?   And yet thou,
Fair Queen of Heaven and Ruler of the seas,
Thou art to-night resplendent and unworn
As when the first man saw thee part the clouds,
And all the stars and planets hid abashed
Before thy majesty!

                      Ah, couldst thou speak,
Could thou but tell us what thine eyes have seen,
How would all human annals pale, and fade
To utter nothingness!   For thou, O Moon,
Thou hast seen all things!   From creation's dawn,
Through night to day, through chaos to the reign
Of peace and order and the sure return
Of season after season, till at length
Earth stood forth radiant in the smile of God,
Thou hast beheld the whole, and watched the growth
Of man from the beginning.   Thou hast seen
The cave-men and the dwellers in the rocks;
And them that dwelt in tents and roamed the plains;
And them that built great cities, proudly fair
With domes and temples, and the stately shrines
Wherein strange gods sat throned in majesty.
And thou hast seen them crumble, stone by stone,
And desert sands drift o'er them till the wolf,
The jackal, and the tiger, reared their young

In the vast solitudes.   Thou didst look on
While Ramses and Sesostris builded high
The mighty pyramids that mock at death,
And when great Thothmes bade the Sphinx keep
   Guard
Forever at the Gate of Mysteries.
Thou hast seen empires rise and empires fall,
And states and kingdoms blossom and decay;
Battle and tumult, and the flaming sword
Blazing before lost Eden—and each night
In every age and every clime new graves!
Earth wearies of them—of her graves that lie
On every hilltop, and in every vale—
For everywhere man dies!

                                            But all unchanged
Thou dost behold the tireless years sweep on,
Seedtime and harvest bringing and the sure
Return of autumn with its golden spoil,
The richest freight in God's great argosies.

....

Silent art thou, O Moon! And on thy face
Dwells immemorial calm, the calm of one
Who sees the end from the beginning.   Thou—
Thou, and Orion , and Alcyone,
And all the stars that gem the midnight heavens—
Ye know that all is well, that Law is Love,
And life and death alike do the Lawgiver's will.

www.ingramcontent.com/pod-product-compliance
Lightning Source LLC
Chambersburg PA
CBHW030137100526
44592CB00011B/935